VINTAGE
Romance

COMIC BOOK COVERS
COLORING BOOK

BOOKS!

IDW PUBLISHING
SAN DIEGO, CALIFORNIA

MW00562196

**Dedicated to our good friend,
Greg Goldstein,
with love.**

—Craig and Clizia

If you like this book, please blog, Facebook, and tweet about it!
Become a fan of YOE Books on Facebook, friend Craig Yoe on Facebook!

Join the Facebook group, "Romance Comics."

ISBN: 978-1-63140-849-6
20 19 18 17 1 2 3 4

Many thanks to our indefatigable friends and experts: Giovanna Anzaldi, Robert Carter, Michelle Nolan, Dave O'Dell.

YoeBooks.com
Craig Yoe & Clizia Gussoni, Chief Executive Officers and Creative Directors • Jeff Trexler, Attorney • Steven Thompson, Publicist.

IDW Publishing
Ted Adams, CEO & Publisher • Greg Goldstein, President & COO • Robbie Robbins, EVP/Sr. Graphic Artist • Chris Ryall, Chief Creative Officer •
David Hedgecock, Editor-in-Chief • Matthew Ruzicka, CPA, Chief Financial Officer • Jeff Webber, VP of Licensing, Digital and Subsidiary Rights •
Jerry Bennington, VP of New Project Development • Dirk Wood, VP of Marketing • Lorelei Bunjes, VP of Digital Services.

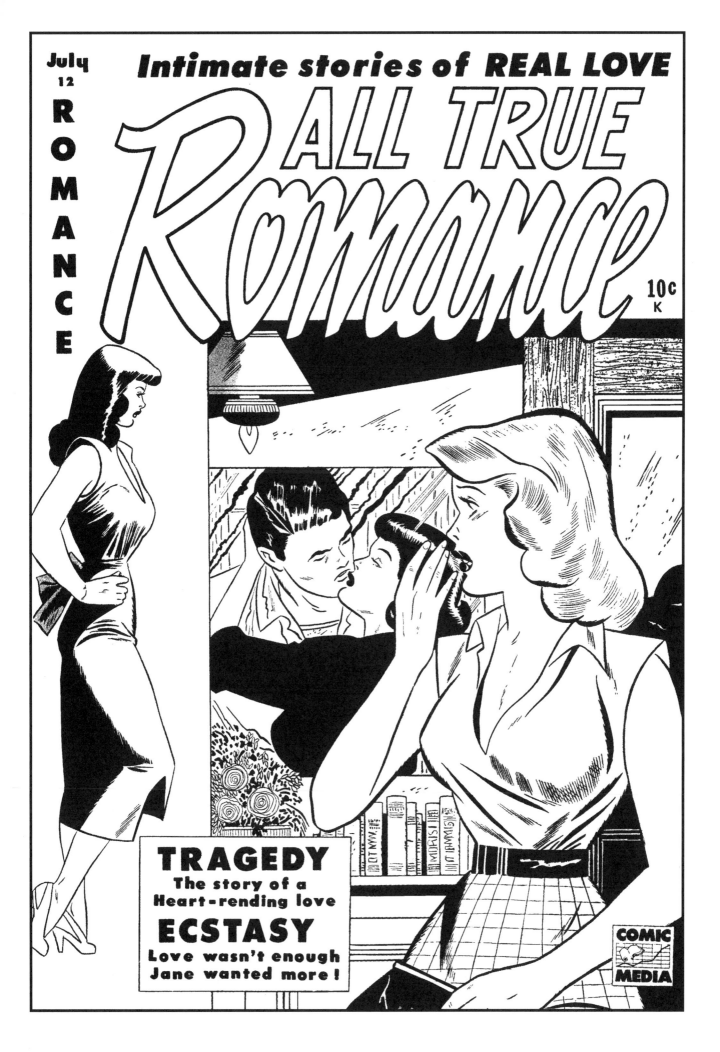

BOY
APRIL NO. 33 10¢
LOVES
GIRL
AUTHORIZED A. C. N. P.
CONFORMS to the COMICS CODE
PDC
LEV GLEASON
INTEGRITY
PUBLICATIONS
I EXCHANGED A FEW MOMENTS OF
BLISS FOR HEARTBREAK AND
DISGRACE!

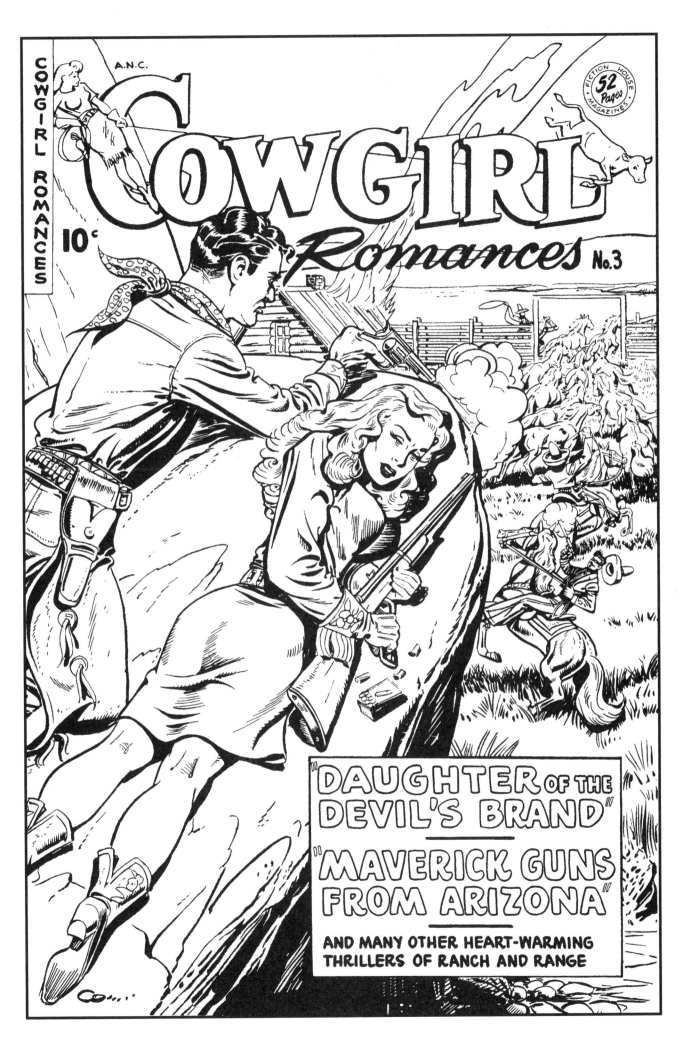

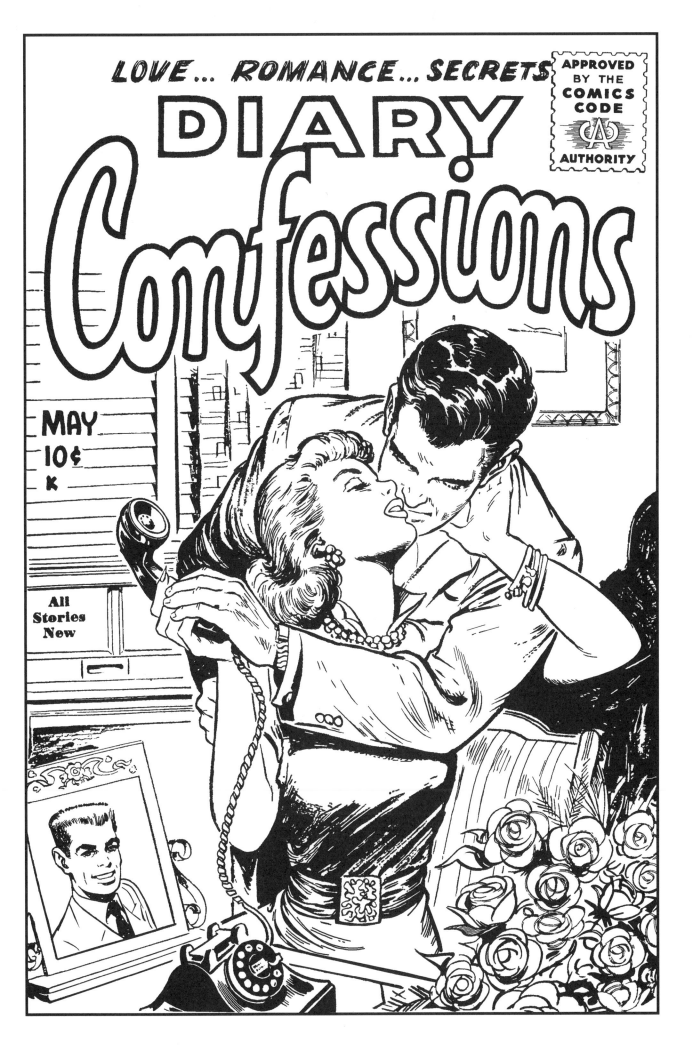

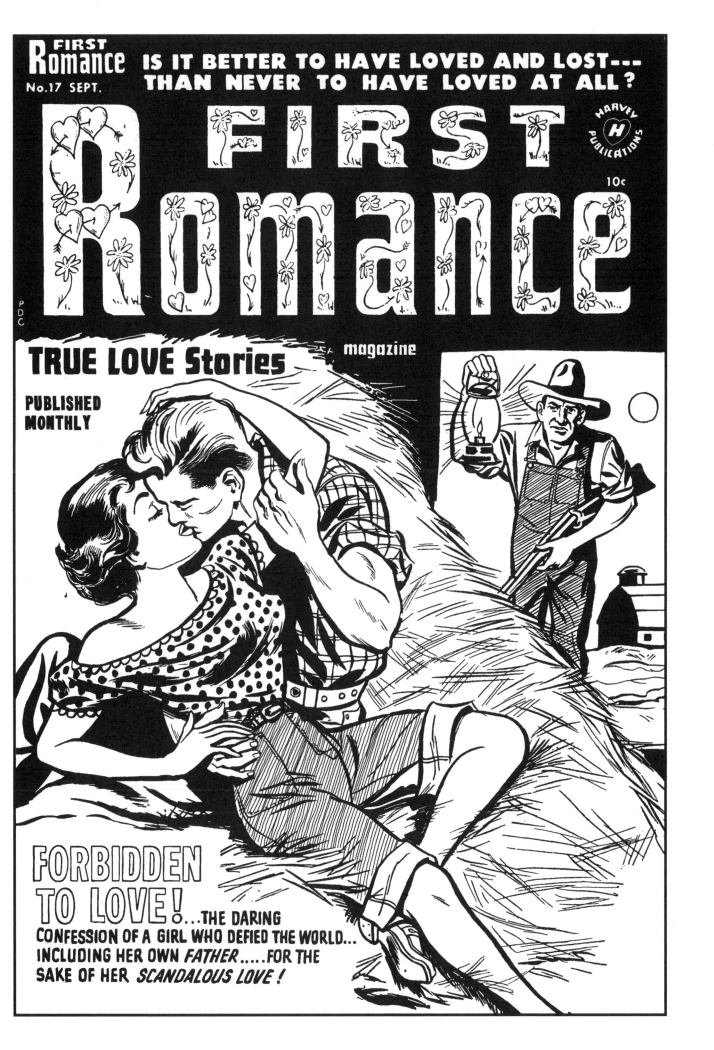

Hi-School Romance

HI-SCHOOL ROMANCE

PBC

TRUE LOVE STORIES

HARVEY PUBLICATIONS

THEY WERE CAUGHT IN THE MERCILESS SPOTLIGHT OF SCANDAL...THE WHOLE TOWN WHISPERED, GOSSIPED, CONDEMNED! *Read* BACKSTAIRS LOVE!

No. 30 JULY 10c

HI-SCHOOL ROMANCE

PDC

Hi-School Romance

TRUE LOVE STORIES

TOO YOUNG TO DOUBT, TOO RECKLESS TO BEWARE, SHE SURRENDERED TO THE SPELL OF HIS....

PORTRAIT OF LOVE

GIANT 52-PAGE SIZE!

Nº 21 - MAY

Romantic Adventures

The MAGAZINE OF YOUTH AND LOVE!

10¢

NICK IS FUN TO BE WITH...AND I DON'T HATE ALL THOSE LOVELY MUSCLES AS MUCH AS I PRETEND!

TRUE LOVE STORIES
TEEN-AGE ROMANCES

THE END